a pagan anti-capitalist primer

Text by Alley Valkyrie & Rhyd Wildermuth

Published by Gods&Radicals

Gods&Radicals
is a non-profit
anti-capitalist
Pagan publisher
and site of Beautiful Resistance.

Find us at godsandradicals.org

Contact us at gods.and.radicals@gmail.com

Resist Beautifully.

You are (most likely) not a Capitalist!

A Capitalist is a specific role and class of people within a society.

Capitalist is a person who invests their money (Capital) by employing people without money (workers) to produce products or services on their behalf.

Under Capitalism, one (small) group of people has money while the rest of the world has to work for them in order to have money.

Who decided that this was going to be way the world should work? Not the gods (though some of the rich certainly have said so). Not Nature or Evolution (though there are some economists and scientists who make a lot of money saying so!). Not the 'will of the people' or Democracy, either—did you ever a get to vote on whether or not you started out life with more money than everyone else?

The answer's kinda obvious, huh? The people with money decided this is the way it should be, because they also had lots of power, massive governments and militaries and sometimes whole religious and ideological institutions were there to serve the Rich, because under Capitalism everything is for sale.

But you're probably not a "Capitalist." You might think it's a good system, or a horrible system, or something in between. You might even never have thought much about it before, and we don't blame you for this, 'cause it's really depressing. But it doesn't matter what you think about Capitalism, because being a Capitalist has nothing to do with how you feel.

Here's a quick checklist to find out if you're a Capitalist

If it turns out you are, don't worry—we won't laugh.

Do you own your own business?
If yes, go to the next question. If NO, you're not a Capitalist.

Do you own a business and pay employees to make money for you?
If No, you're not a Capitalist
If yes?
Congratulations! You're a Capitalist!

You can be a poor Capitalist, by the way, though the goal is to be a rich one. There are plenty of tiny business owners who employ only one or two people to make stuff on their behalf, or ring up sales or watch a desk for a while and don't make much money. Some of them are often not much better off than their workers, except for one very important thing the owner (the Capitalist) gets to decide how much to pay workers and gets to keep all the profit.

If it turns out you are a Capitalist, have hope! And keep reading.

And you're not, *this primer is especially for you.*

> "Advocates of capitalism are very apt to appeal to the
> sacred principles of liberty, which are embodied in
> one maxim: The fortunate must not be restrained in
> the exercise of tyranny over the unfortunate."
> -Bertrand Russell

So, I'm Not A Capitalist...
What Am I, Then?

Ugh, sorry. You're a worker, part of what Anarchists and Marxists call The Proletariat.

But don't worry. *So are we.* You're not alone—actually, we're all subjects of Capitalism, even the Capitalists themselves. But...we suffer a bit more.

Being a worker means you've got no access to the means of production, which is just a weird way of saying that you can't make a living without working for someone else.

Ever have the feeling when you don't have a job and have no money and feel like you've suddenly become a pariah to society? A nobody? Almost invisible and definitely "useless?" This is because you've got no means of your own production.

This is never 100% true, though. You can always grow your own food—that is, if you can find enough land to do it on. But of course, there are laws against turning other people's land into farms, because of an essential aspect of Capitalism Private Property

We don't mean personal property, like your clothes and food and Book of Shadows. We mean Land Ownership, which is a very new idea that came about right at the time Capitalism started.

Coincidence? No. Not at all.

Lots of Pagan religions like the earth and believe in spirits, faeries, and gods of land, or in a great earth spirit or mother or goddess. That's one of the reasons why Paganism is usually defined as an 'earth-based' religion.

And who can own the land or the trees? Well, under Capitalism, the people with money and power and access to the systems that delegate and enforce private property rights. Everyone else has to stay off; in fact, **Private Property** demands 'exclusion' from the land (think No Trespassing signs...).

And that unequal relationship to the land is essential to Capitalism, because it prevents workers from ever making a living in any other way except working for the Capitalists.

"The essence of capitalism is to turn nature into commodities and commodities into capital. The live green earth is transformed into dead gold bricks, with luxury items for the few and toxic slag heaps for the many. The glittering mansion overlooks a vast sprawl of shanty towns, wherein a desperate, demoralized humanity is kept in line with drugs, television, and armed force."
-Michael Parenti

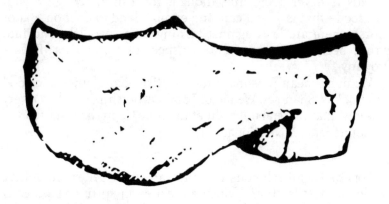

Workers (Co-)Create the World

Because we were just telling you about all the depressing things that come with being a worker instead of a Capitalist, it's probably a good idea to tell you about what's kinda good about being a worker.

First of all— *we do all the work.*

No, really. We do. Occasionally, you might hear your boss or manager talking about how they're really important and without them the company will fall apart. Don't believe 'em—they just tell those stories to re-assure themselves.

Consider a smartphone. Who's responsible for that thing, the Corporation who sells it or the hundreds and hundreds of people who write the software, design the electronics, and labor away in factories putting it together?

Or take a cup of coffee. Who's responsible for the latte you drink in the morning, the owner of the cafe or the barista who made it, the people who roasted the beans, and the people who grew it?

And now ask yourself one more thing—who gets all the extra money from your purchase of the latte or the smartphone?

Certainly, not the people who actually made the thing.

The only part of the process that the Capitalist is involved in is the investment of Capital. That is, the Capitalist builds the cafe or starts the business and invests their money in order to make more money.

One of the most common excuses you'll hear from an owner as to why they deserve to keep all the extra money for themselves is because "it's me who's taking all the risks."

Sounds fair, right? But consider the consequences if their business fails, if their risk doesn't pan out. What happens to them? They'll have no access to the means of production anymore, and be forced to become a worker, instead.

That is, they risk becoming one of us. Even they know our position is horrible and wouldn't want to be us.

All The World Is Owned

"Capitalism is the legitimate racket of the ruling class."
-Al Capone

So, Capitalism is a system where some people get to own businesses and companies and factories (the means of production) and get out of the cycle of work, while the rest of us have to sell our time in the form of labor in order to survive. Doesn't seem so fair, huh?

Yet there are plenty of ways where we justify this system anyway. Before we get into more detail about the way Capitalism works, let's look at those justifications, shall we?

Capitalism is (not) a 'Natural' system

We tend to think of the study of economics as one of the so-called 'Hard Sciences' because there are numbers, figures, and measures involved. Modern ways of describing the economy like Gross Domestic Product, Un-employment figures, or Inflation, at first all appear to be scientific measures of natural phenomenon like Radioactive Decay, Velocity, or Cell-division.

What both Economics and the physical sciences share is the use of statistics to measure and describe things, but Economics describes a particularly Human activity, one that, though someone predictable, is not a 'Natural' force.

That is, unlike the laws of gravitational pull or thermodynamics, Economics describes something we actually have control over, behaviors and activities which are not immutable and eternal. As far as we can tell, gravity has always been mostly constant throughout time and Natural Selection has generally behaved in similar ways over the aeons of life on Earth. However, Economic activity is not constant, nor has it ever been, and as opposed to gravity or thermodynamics, there is not a single agreed-upon understanding of how economics and Capitalism work, despite what many want you to believe.

While some theorists have attempted to show that Capitalism was a 'natural' or even 'evolutionary' inevitability, this is no different from suggesting that your birth was inevitable. It's a post hoc ('after the fact') explanation that is not much different from Calvinist ideas of Predestination and Providence, the faith that the Present was 'supposed' to happen. It's an insidious framework that's been used to justify all manner of horrific things, including American Imperialism (Manifest Destiny) and Slavery (1800's-era Social Darwinism).

Capitalism has (not) always been around.

This, more than anything, is often the greatest difficulty many of us have when attempting to understand Capitalism. Capitalism has not always existed; in fact, it's been around for no more than 350 years.

Capitalism started sometime in the 1700's as a specifically new economic arrangement quite different from those which came before. Those other systems were not necessarily better or worse than Capitalism, but they were different enough that they represent completely different social arrangements.

Precisely when Capitalism started is difficult to say. On a long enough scale, we can point to the 1500's and 1600's and say, no—there was no Capitalism during that time, and look at the 1800's and say, yes, that's Capitalism. It's much the same difficulty historians have deciding precisely when a war begins or ends. Did World War I start with the assassination of Archduke Ferdinand, or with the first declaration of war or when the last 'great power' entered? And World War II—did that start when the US declared war on Germany, or on Japan? And did it end when treaties were signed or when the last bullet was shot?

One thing we know for certain. Capitalism-as-we-know-it was born in England.

Capitalism is (not) Democratic

"In the Soviet Union, capitalism triumphed over communism. In this country, capitalism triumphed over democracy."
-Fran Lebowitz

The capitalist system, as illustrated by International Worker

CAPITALISM

WE RULE YOU

WE FOOL YOU

WE SHOOT YOU

WE EAT FOR YOU

WE WORK FOR ALL

WE FEED ALL

PYRAMID of CAPITALIST SYSTEM

Most people know this, but it bears repeating because of what is inculcated through our educational, political, and media institutions. Democracy is a political form, a method of governance distinct from economic activities. Capitalism is a form of Economic arrangement, distinct from governance.

A nation can be Democratic and Capitalist or Democratic and non-Capitalist. There have been and still are non-Democratic Capitalist countries, such as Chile under the US-installed General Augusto Pinochet. Also, China, by most estimations, uses a non-Democratic "State-Capitalist" system, though this is debatable.

We should keep in mind, though, that certain economic systems rely on political backup. Communism, for instance, requires a strong central government, which is why it tends towards totalitarianism. Capitalism requires strong property-laws and harsh enforcement of those laws in order to function.

Because of this, Capitalists tend to prefer any governmental system in which they have a greater say than their workers, and this often causes those governmental systems to become less-democratic over time.

In fact, Capitalism needs inequality, which is the antithesis of democratic governance.

Capitalism Creates (in)Equality

"No person, I think, ever saw a herd of buffalo, of which a few were fat and the great majority lean. No person ever saw a flock of birds, of which two or three were swimming in grease, and the others all skin and bone."
--Henry George

One of the most insidious things about Capitalism is that it cannot abide equality. As a matter of fact, it needs to prevent it at every point.

If everyone is paid the same amount for the work they do, then Capitalists cannot force workers to compete against each other. That competition is essential to keeping wages down as low as possible so that profit stays as high as it can get.

Competition occurs in nature, but so does co-operation. Humans certainly compete with each other, but without co-operation, we wouldn't live in villages, towns, and cities, wouldn't trade with each other, or even figure out how to have sex with each other without violence.

But Capitalism requires, fosters, encourages, and even artificially creates competition, especially between groups of workers. Workers who co-operate can make demands together, and a group of 40 people against one boss is much more powerful than 40 individuals all out for their own survival.

On a larger scale, Capitalism benefits from and often exacerbates sexism, racism, and xenophobia. We know that women get paid less than men, and we usually ascribe this to the patriarchy. But we forget that an owner benefits from this inequality—he or she can pay women a little less then men and thus get cheaper labor from them. Women, immigrants, and non-whites are often shunted into very low wage work (home health-care, textiles, housecleaning, fast-food service), and because they have less political power, owners are able to keep their wages low (and thus sustain very high profits in those industries).

But if you look at white men in the 'lower-classes,' you'll find an odd thing. Even as they are also getting exploited, many of them tend towards racist and sexist thinking. Many poor and unemployed white men will blame 'the immigrants' for their own poverty, and will distrust or actively hate people of other racists.

Not only is this quite useful to the Capitalists, but its actually exacerbated and encouraged. If you've got a TV, go watch an hour or two of any news program and count how many stories there are about black crime or illegal immigrants. It's almost difficult to not be a little racist after this!

> **"You can't have capitalism without racism."**
> **Malcolm X**

Then, remind yourself who owns those broadcasters, who funds those broadcasts, and who might benefit from poor people hating other poor people.

Capitalism is (not) 'Progress'

"Every benefit industrialism and capitalism have
brought us, every wonderful advance in knowledge
and health and communication and comfort, casts the
same fatal shadow. All we have, we have taken from
the earth; and, taking with ever-increasing speed and
greed, we now return little but what is sterile or
poisoned."
-Ursula K. LeGuin

In the 1700's, right around the time of the Birth of Capitalism, an interesting and very unhelpful idea was born, which we'll call The Progress Narrative.

Think about it for a moment—are you better off now than you might have been a thousand years ago? Five hundred years ago? Or even 100 years ago?

The answer is typically, 'yes, of course,' citing longer life-spans, refrigerators, dentistry, or the end of slavery as things we have now that make life better than what it was. But we tend not to speak of the fact that life is not better for all, that indentured servitude still exists amongst migrant workers in the United States, and that slavery still exists over the world, including in many 'Capitalist' countries. We especially don't like to acknowledge or think about the fact that most of the consumer products and many of the food products we buy every day are touched by slavery at some point in the supply chain.

Nor do we often speak of quality of life and free-time. Peasants in the middle ages, for instance, often worked 100 days fewer per year than we do, had access to fresher foods (and thus no need for refrigerators) and a lack of processed sugars in the diets (again, peasants often died with very good teeth.

But rather than get into the specific ways that things may not necessarily be 'better' than before, it's more important to look at 'why' we have the belief that the present is better than the past. This is very, very new idea, birthed during the Enlightenment alongside Capitalism and one of the major engines of Capitalist development, Improvement.

Adam Smith was the first philosopher to develop an idea of

'improvement' as a basic requirement for human society, and for him it applied primarily to land and production. In fact, one of the arguments he provided to British colonialists to justify the murder and theft of land from Native Americans was that they were not doing anything with the land; that is, they weren't 'improving' it.

Improvement is the primary imperative of Capitalism, because the Capitalist always wants to make more money (produce more) from their Capital. Improvements in production like assembly-line manufacture were created specifically to lower labor costs and increase profit.

> "Comforts that were rare among our forefathers are now multiplied in factories and handed out wholesale; and indeed, nobody nowadays, so long as he is content to go without air, space, quiet, decency and good manners, need be without anything whatever that he wants; or at least a reasonably cheap imitation of it."
> -G. K. Chesterton

Capitalism Encourages Technological Advance (...or you starve)

The need to improve production is certainly so great that it seems like Capitalism increases the rate of technological development. But we should remember something—every engineer, every medical researcher, ever scientist is operating under the same imperative that a barista or a janitor is under work or starve.

In essence, the logic of Capitalism is the logic of a labor camp, with guards, managers and even cameras posted in some businesses to make sure you're productive. Often, though, it doesn't need these safeguards, because you already know what will happen if you don't produce what your boss wants you to you'll be jobless, and thus poor and perhaps homeless and hungry.

Likewise, though there have been all sorts of amazing scientific and technological advances in the last two centuries (first satellite in space!...oh, wait...), these advances are rarely available to everyone unless they'll turn a profit for the company that holds the patent. Ask HIV+ Africans about how readily accessible anti-retroviral medication is, or ask your doctor how much cancer treatment will cost you.

This is certainly 'technological advance,' but it is not ever for everyone.

Also, there's a funny thing that happens, noted by David Graeber in his essay "On Flying Cars and the Declining Rate of Profit." The need to make money off of an invention will actually prevent money going towards 'wild ideas' and instead towards things that are very, very similar to what's already around. Worse, some advances are specifically stifled, like high-efficiency transport and long-lasting lightbulbs. Things that last longer and use less resources are actually bad for Capitalism.

Ask yourself why Capitalism hasn't 'figured out' how to make a laptop fan that doesn't die after two years, and if you get a chance, go see the Centennial Light Bulb, first turned on in 1901. It's still working.

> Capitalist production, therefore, develops technology,
> and the combining together of various processes into
> a social whole, only by sapping the original sources of
> all wealth—the soil and the labourer."
> -Karl Marx

What Exactly is Capitalism?

Capitalism is a social arrangement where the majority of people in any society have only one way to make a living by working for others.

Consider your own situation. Unless you are independently wealthy, you probably have a job. In fact, you need to have one in order to pay rent and buy food, two things which are essential to your survival.

If you don't have a job, you don't get money, and if you don't have money, you can't eat or pay rent. That is, you'll starve and be homeless unless you've got friends to stay with and either get food assistance from the government or go to a food bank.

It could be said, then, that you don't actually have a choice you must have a job.

Now, let's look at the people you work for. They may be really nice people, and maybe you're fortunate enough to work for the government or a non-profit agency where there's no profit motive. These jobs are few and rare and more often than not end up serving Capitalists in some way or another.

The vast majority of us, though, take jobs for business, companies, and corporations who are out to make money by making or selling products. A coder who works at Microsoft, a barista at a coffeeshop, a migrant worker in the fields, and an assembly-line worker in a factory are all in the exact same position—they are making things for their bosses to sell. That is, they are all Producers, but they do not get the full 'value' of the product they produce.

A tech-professional might create an app for their company that makes millions, but the person or people who created it only get paid salary. A barista might sell 100 dollars worth of coffee (or 60 dollars after 'overhead' is subtracted), but still only makes minimum wage+tips. A migrant worker might pick 60 lbs of tomatoes but still only earn $20 for them, and a factory worker might, in a week, make items the factory owner sells for $1000, but the worker only makes $400 in a week.

The extra money (after 'production costs'--keeping the lights on in a cafe, paying rent on a factory, insurance and advertising and regulation fees) is called Profit, and in almost all cases, the owner of the business gets to keep all of this.

But some workers are paid more than others....

In the example above, we said a migrant worker and a computer coder are in the same position. This is true, but also not completely. Some workers are paid more in a Capitalist system than others. To hear the media and business owners speak to this, one gets the impression that some people are just worth more than others, or at least their work is. And...this is true, at least as far as they're concerned.

How much a Capitalist pays a worker is dependent on many factors, including the skill and training of certain workers, but we shouldn't let ourselves fall into the modern lie of "Meritocracy," the idea that higher-paid workers somehow 'deserve' more money than lower paid workers.

If you've ever watched a janitor, a farm-worker, or construction worker do their jobs, it's awfully hard to say that they 'deserve less pay' than someone who sits at a desk in front of a computer all day. And pay isn't dependent upon necessity to the system, either—a trash-collector might make $20/hour, while an advertising agent might make 5 times that amount. That trash-collector is keeping plague and pestilence from spreading throughout a city, while the advertiser is only helping sell a product.

In fact, the more basic and vital a job seems to be to the survival and health of a society, the less they seem to get paid. The farm workers who grow and pick your food, the EMTs who transport your bleeding body from an automobile accident to the Emergency Room, social workers who help prevent suicides and mental-health related crimes, and health-care workers who keep the elderly alive in nursing facilities all make less than the median wage in the area they live in. Meanwhile, IT professionals, software designers, and film producers make many, many, many times this amount.

Capitalism values one and only one thing in a worker how much money that worker will 'produce' for the owner. A janitor doesn't produce a product, an EMT doesn't make something 'to sell,' and a social worker will never make money for the agency they work for.

The prime directive of a Capitalist is always and only 'to

Profit' from other people's effort. The person behind the Capitalist might be a great person, might really care about the environment or their workers, but these all must come secondary to the need to make money. The kind, eco-friendly Capitalist is, in the end, not much different from the handful of 'humane' slave-owners in the ante-bellum south, or as Oscar Wilde said,

> *"...the worst slave-owners were those who were kind to their slaves, and so prevented the horror of the system being realised by those who suffered from it, and understood by those who contemplated it"*

Capitalism Versus Paganism

So we come to the question of why a Pagan should care about Capitalism at all. Why, after all, should a group of people worshiping gods and nature care about what sort of economic system we've got? To understand this, we need to look at precisely how Capitalism came about, what it requires, what it does to people and the earth, and what it will always get in the way of.

(graphic by www.prole.info)

The Birth of Capitalism

As we said previously, Capitalism started in England sometime during the 1700's. Most historians point to the Enclosure of the Commons as the most significant event which created the economic system we now know (and despise), so it's worth looking at what that was and what changed.

Previous to the Enclosure Acts passed by the English parliament in the 1700's, land was not a commodity (that is, something to be bought or sold on the open market). Land wasn't really a 'thing' to be owned by most people, nor something you could suddenly lose access to except by force.

In Feudal villages throughout Europe, land was held by lords who laid claim to it through ancestral 'right', previous violence (wars, mostly), receipt from kings or other lords (through marriage or as gifts from Monarchs for service), or, in some very rare cases, purchase or trade between other lords.

Peasants and serfs (that is, the vast majority of humans) lived either on land claimed by lords (that is, landed-lords or 'land-lords,' for short...funny we still use that term, huh?), in independent towns or villages, or on land claimed by a king but not directly ruled. Those peasants who lived in Feudal arrangements were required to give over 1/3rd (remember this percentage!) of the food they grew on their lord's land in return for protection—an early form of 'protection racket.'

Feudal lords couldn't kick people off of their land except for specific reasons outlined by custom and tradition ('common-law'), and these reasons were typically for failure to pay the 1/3rd due to the lord. Outside of those reasons, serfs had established 'right' to work and live on the land where they lived and a right to everything else they produced except church tithes (10%). Serfs, peasants, townsfolk and artisans sold their extra to each other in markets which were nothing like Capitalist markets now. In fact, there were common-law provisions about excess profit-taking, and in the example of the many bread-riots in the 18th and 19th centuries, one can see that there was a universal idea of how much something 'should' cost.

In fact, let's look at the bread riots for a moment, because they're a great way to understand how society and values have changed because of Capitalism.

Bread And Roses

The word 'riot' sounds pretty terrifying, huh? Sometimes they're fun, and sometimes often carnivalesque.

It was a very common thing, during the beginning of Industrialized Capitalism, for these events to occur as prices for wheat flour became subject to Capitalist 'market logic' instead of tradition and custom.

They went like this Bakers (often men) who had to pay much more for their flour than usual would attempt to adjust prices for their bread accordingly. Customers, often women, would decide that the prices were too high and would refuse to pay them. However, as opposed to the modern logic that says 'if you can't afford it, you can't have it,' these groups of women would organize together and crowd into the bake shops. But instead of stealing bread, they'd do a very strange thing they'd tie up the baker and then begin selling the bread to each other at the previous 'fair price.' The baker still got money (and often a beating from the angry women, a way to punish him for trying to take more than what was fair) and the women got their bread.

Now, if such a thing were to happen, the women would all be imprisoned or shot by riot police.

Before Capitalism, there was a sense that excess-profit was a bad thing. This wasn't just come from religion or mere moralism. Instead, people had a greater sense of inter-connectedness, of community, and of mutual aid and responsibility. By charging more than people could afford, the bakers were choosing profit over the well-being of people in their community, and folks rioted in response.

Also, many of the leaders of such riots were women. In fact, many of the changes in society caused by Capitalism affected women directly. There's a very deep connection between the subjugation of women and the birth of Capitalism, and it's no co-incidence that the period just before Capitalism started, Europe was wracked with witch-hunts. Capitalism would have been impossible without first subjugating women, just as it also needed to subjugate Blacks and Indigenous peoples.

"These Satanic Mills"

With Capitalism came Industrialization, the worst thing that has ever happened to Nature.

Industrialization is the process of organizing human labor in such a way that productivity goes as high as possible with human input becoming minimal. The 'promise' of industrialization was that workers would need to put in less time to make products, and humans would have more free time. But it never, ever happened this way, because the excess profits derived from factory labor and automation wasn't shared with the workers, it went to the owners.

In the late 1700's, a man named James Watts figured out how to run machines by super-heating water with burning coal. This invention, the 'steam engine,' wildly increased the pace of industrialization while also increasing damage to the planet through human activity.

Coal, and then oil, were readily available, didn't go on strike, didn't ask for time off, and didn't talk back when the owners demanded they do more work. In fact, Coal and Oil seemed the quintessential replacement worker, readily available and very easy to abuse.

But we know, of course, that burning coal and oil release toxins into the atmosphere, but it was an invisible limit on human activity, one that took several centuries to become obvious. Humans could only work for so long, forests could only grow so fast —there were 'natural' and easily understood limits on human production. With Oil and Coal, there seemed to be no limit to Capitalist expansion, until the earth started heating up and the oceans started rising.

Once, humans made contracts with the land and the gods for sovereignty. Take too much and the land revolted with famine or pestilence. Industrialized Capitalism seemed to be an escape from these 'Natural' laws and relationship to the earth, but as the ice-caps melt, it's pretty obvious the Earth cannot be overcome.

> "Growth for the sake of growth is the ideology of the
> cancer cell."
> -Edward Abbey

Capitalism requires both infinite growth and infinite resources, which conflicts with the simple fact that our resources on this planet are finite and that abusively depleting those resources affects the health and well-being of all life forms on this planet as well as the planet itself.

Capitalism is a system which always takes more than it gives back. We can see this in modern agriculture, where the use of chemical fertilizers is essential to grow food now, because so much land has been spoiled and stripped. Coal and oil are running out, water sources depleted, mountains leveled and forests razed.

It does this to nature, and this does this to nature's creatures, including humans. What is left for us at the end of 45 years of work? We have little to show except our salaries, and these are always smaller than the amount of 'value' we created for our owners. We are like forests and the sea, always giving more to the Capitalists than they give back, and we are ever dwindling in our strength, magic, and life until we finally die and nothing can be taken from us any longer.

While we are just trying to 'make a living,' they are always trying to 'make a killing.'

It's not just a horrible system, it's a cruel system, and we enact its cruelty upon each other. Capitalism is a social arrangement, and it alters are relationships to each other. The world is disenchanted, or as Marx and Engles said,

> "Everything that is solid melts into air, everything sacred is profaned...."

We Pagans are trying to re-enchant the world, to bring back the magic of the forests and the mountains. We are trying to hear and revere the wild places, the sacred forgotten places, the spirits of ocean and rivers and lakes. And yet Capitalism is always poisoning these places because it considers nothing sacred except profit, nothing holy except wealth.

> "We have disenchanted ourselves, handed over our teeth and claws and bristling luxuriant furs. I will not be part of this process, because to do so is to be complicit with the very forces that are destroying all life on earth. It is time for Witchcraft not to choose, but to remember which side it is on in this struggle."
> *Peter Grey,* "Rewilding Witchcraft"

To Re-Enchant the World, we must destroy Capitalism. And we're not alone—indigenous peoples on every continent have been trying to do this for centuries, and it's not surprise that they revere the earth and gods and each other in ways that Capitalism cannot abide and Capitalism must destroy.

An Other World Is Possible

"We live in capitalism the way people in Russia lived in dictatorship. It's our whole world. You can't get outside capitalism at this point, but you can ... well, you can subvert it, or you can find ways through and out, which is what I think the arts ... they always lead through and out of situations. The arts always give a pathway of "it doesn't have to be exactly like this, and it won't be like this forever."
- *Ursula K. LeGuin*

The most common questions we get from people after explaining how horrible, destructive, and really mean Capitalism can be, is 'what next?' What do we do about it?

It's difficult to answer this question as an anarchist. One of the primary tenets of Anarchism is that no one should ever have power-over anyone else, nor should anyone tell anyone else what to do. Thus, being asked "what should I do?" presents a huge problem for us.

Also, there's another matter. Grand programs and one-size-fits-all solutions don't work. Soviet and Chinese Communism both operated this way, and besides the many other problems they caused, the one-size-fits-all model led to massacres, gulags, and wars.

One answer cannot possibly fit every single one of the almost 8 billion people sharing this planet with us. Anyone who does come up with that answer should probably be shot on sight, as they're pretty likely gonna start shooting people themselves pretty soon. Besides, 'one-answer' sounds a lot like one-god, and we Pagans have lots of reason to be rue that one-god trend.

That being said, here's some places to start. Neither of us can overthrow Capitalism on our own, nor can a small group of people. Even if one million of us all gathered together to overthrow the corporations, without something already in place to fulfill the needs those corporations profit from meeting, more will just spring up in their place.

Getting rid of Capitalism will take many, many people, and many different forms of resistance. Some of this may be just starting organic farms in alleys in cities, or creating mutual-aid groups across regions and countries. Some of this will involve direct resistance and even violence. That's scary, and we'd really like to think that won't need to happen. But judging from recent human history and how desperate the rich have been to hold onto power and wealth, we won't lie to you—they're gonna get violent.

We're not advocating violent overthrow of the government, nor mass beheadings of CEO's of oil companies. And anyway, those in power have a monopoly on violence—they can always do more violence to us than we could ever do to them. Smashing the window of a corporate coffee-chain location can never compare to the bombings, assassinations, mass-imprisonments, and all-out wars that have occurred whenever people actively resist. We can't beat them at these escalations.

What we can do, however, is something more radical and beautiful. We can begin to create the world we want to see now so that, as Capitalism begins to break apart, we're ready to take over, like chamomile growing in the cracks of pavement.

Build Community—Yesterday

"We are nothing if we walk alone, we are everything when we walk together in step with other dignified feet." Subcomandante Marcos

Capitalism has caused the destruction of community in every place it's taken root. As a matter of fact, it needs to do this, since alienation is one of the mechanisms it uses to keep workers and consumers competing against each other, rather than co-operating.

People who co-operate with each other learn to trust each other and are more likely to help each other through 'extra-economic' means. Consider let's say you catch a really nasty flu. You cannot go to work, you cannot take care of yourself, you can't make yourself food or do things for your children.

If you have no community, you must rely on 'the market' for

your needs. You would have to hire someone to watch your children, order food delivered to your door, and you'll find yourself spending even more money than you might have if you were well. It may also take you longer to feel better.

This same situation changes radically if you are part of a community. When you let friends, family, and neighbors know that you are ill, they naturally offer to help. A relative might offer to watch your children for a few days, neighbors might bring you food, friends might go pick up medicine for you and come by to help you tidy your place or watch movies with you. And the most radical thing of all? None of them would even think to charge you for these 'services.'

Communities like this don't spring up overnight—they take years to cultivate. They can't be bought, and if they're strong enough and communicate well, they can't be bought-out. Groups of neighbors fighting against developers or polluters, building community gardens and co-operative child-care networks are all essential ways of resisting.

But in building these communities, there is a danger we must constantly be vigilant about. If you are a middle-class white person living in a middle-class white suburb, the tendency to fear those who don't 'fit in' can be very dangerous. Not all communities are radical; sometimes (as in the South during segregation or even some of the supposedly 'liberal' areas of the Northwest), these community networks can be outright racist.

This brings us to the next suggestion.

Make Common Cause With Others

It is not always easy to see how a struggle in one place might relate to a struggle somewhere else, but it's essential if we're to over-grow the monoculture of Capitalism.

In Dublin in December, 2014, there were massive street demonstrations against the Irish Government's attempt to increase the cost of water and eventually privatize water distribution. The organizers of these protests paid for a delegation of people from an American city to speak as guests of honor, and their presence may seem surprising at first, but shouldn't be at all. The group? The Detroit Water Brigade, an activist group who's been fighting the same battle in their own city. Standing in front of thousands of Irish folk were a small group, many of them African-American, making common cause with people fighting against profit-taking for basic human services!

Making these sorts of connections across cultural, racial, ethnic, religious and political boundaries is both beautiful and vital, as the alienation that Capitalism requires is enforced by fear, hatred, racism, and homophobia. In fact, it is in the best interest of Capitalists and the governments who support them to ensure the poor never find common cause. Anti-immigrant sentiment amongst unemployed white working-class men, for instance, prevents two groups of economically powerless workers do not unite against the employers who play them against each other.

> "The secret of managing is to keep the guys who hate you away from the guys who are undecided."
> -Casey Stengel

The struggle against Capitalism has been going on ever since it began, and Paganism has been a crucial element of this. Other indigenous religions, likewise, fight the same battles that Europeans lost in the 1700's, and many of these struggles are on-going and even just starting. Also, there are allies in places we forget to look. Many non-Western Buddhist leaders have fought against it, and there are entire strands of Monotheist theology devoted to ending Capitalism (see particularly Liberation Theology).

Make common cause as much as possible, across every racial, ethnic, political, and religious background you can. Find ways to support similar struggles in other countries, on indigenous land in the Americas, and in your own cities and towns. While building community around you, always look for ways to connect your community to other communities, even (and especially!) if those people appear to look and act nothing like you. Resist Capitalist alienation by resisting personal alienation.

Invest in Each Other, Divest From Capitalism

If you own stock (whether through a 401k/403b or other retirement fund, or through a benefit program from your employer), you are invested in the success of Capitalism. That is, you need Capitalism to continue and those companies you own stock in to profit, otherwise you lose your money and face poverty in retirement.

If Capitalism fails, you lose.

Tricky, huh? And awfully insidious. And stock-ownership isn't the only way we become invested in the perpetuation of Capitalism. Home ownership is another one when you buy a home, you are not just tied to a mortgage but also the success of the employer you work for. You now need your employer to do well, to turn a profit, to continue to pay you regularly (and a little more each year), otherwise you will lose your home.

It's a trap, and it was actually designed this way. In the early half of the 20th century, with the threat of civil revolt always on the minds of politicians, economists and theorists pointed out that home-owners were less likely to go on strike, because they would not risk losing their jobs and their homes. This realization resulted in a political push to increase home-ownership in the United States, rather than follow the European pattern of home-rental (Switzerland, for instance, with a higher standard of living than the US, has half the home-ownership rate of the US).

There are many, many more ways in which we 'invest' ourselves in the perpetuation of Capitalism. Sometimes these are not our fault, other times they are. Our life choices and desired 'standard of living' have much to do with how much we'll need

Capitalism to succeed. If we think we need a swimming pool and two cars to be happy, we'll definitely need the companies we work for to succeed.

If we need less, we have less to lose, which is why the poor are always more likely to revolt than the middle-classes.

Do you have credit cards? If so, do you really need them? Credit and debt not only benefit capitalism, but purchasing items that you don't really need on credit keeps you forever tied to the system.

Do you keep your money in a bank? If so, why? Banks are for-profit institutions that use your money to make more money off the very systems that are destroying our ability to live on this planet. Credit unions, on the other hand, perform the same functions as banks but are non-profit institutions that keep your money in the community. The bank needs you much more than you need the bank. Ditching the bank is a small but significant divestment from capitalism.

Look at your income from your employer as your buy-out. Your salary is not just how much your boss has decided your time is worth, but the bare minimum required to keep you from steal-ing from them, or sabotaging the machines. Consider that wage and ask yourself—is that how much it really costs for your com-plicity? It's probably not enough, even if it's more than other people are getting.

Consume Less, Create More

Related to the last point, consider how much you consume versus how much you actually create. This is also a hard one, and the consequences will be different for each per-son. We should try to avoid two traps here, that of ethical con-sumption and 'Puritanical Guilt.' Both of these are related to each other.

Do you try to buy organic foods? Non-damaging cleaning products, hybrid or electric cars? What about fair-trade coffee, or non-sweatshop-made garments? Do you try to buy local?

These are all good, and they also won't do a damn thing by themselves. If anything, they resemble certain Christian values, those of personal abstention and individual purity being the way 'to heaven.'

Consuming better doesn't end the problem of Capitalism. Worse, ethical consumption has become a marketing ploy. Companies like Starbucks create entire lines of products for people hoping to do less damage to the earth and others, while still making 'a killing' on their non-ethical, non-greenwashed products. A brief look at the packaging in the organic aisles of a corporate grocery store like Whole Foods, for instance, will make it pretty clear—they're marketing to your desire for a better world, and charging you extra just for the privilege.

This isn't to say we shouldn't try to be more ethical about our consumption, only that we need a healthy dose of cynicism and a sober helping of realism here. An organic apple won't save the planet from global warming; an end to Capitalist production will.

So, when looking at your consumption habits, always keep in mind that anything you buy through the Capitalist system sustains, supports, and perpetuates Capitalism, no matter the product. Consume as little of these things as you can, and learn to create what the market sells back to you.

Cooking for yourself is more radical than buying an organic frozen dinner or eating at a local restaurant specifically because it is a non-economic activity. Cooking for others? Even better (and endless fun). There are many, many, many things are grandparents and ancestors did for themselves that we no longer do (and often have forgotten how to or even that we can!). Those things are the stuff of life and community. Sewing circles, group meals, community gardens, barn raisings, festivals, craft-faires.

We don't need to provide everything ourselves. Actually, we cannot, and never have in the history of humanity. This is why we live in villages and tribes and towns and cities and families. The modern Libertarian frontier fantasy is just that—a fantasy. And besides, turning 7 billion people out into the forests to forage on their own will destroy the forests right quick.

By creating what we consume and creating for others to consume, we create economies outside Capitalism. Remember—markets, buying, and selling aren't Capitalist until someone starts making a profit off of someone else's misery.

Resist Often and Everywhere

Capitalism infects all of our social relationships, so every social relationship is a potential place of Revolution.

Consider the way you 'value' your friends and experiences with them. Do you sometimes calculate what can be gotten from them versus what you return? You learned this from Capitalism. You should unlearn it.

Think about your relationship to the place you live. Is it a place you 'use' or is it a world you inhabit and cherish and care for?

Consider the way you look at strangers. Do you fear them, or try to see the divine in them? Resist fear at every opportunity, and build trust. Remember, competition and fear are central tenets of Capitalism, and the opposite of them is Love and Joy.

Look at the ways other people resist. Do you judge them? Consider questions of theft and property-damage, or the workers who slack off. Remember that most crimes are 'property' crimes, and owners are trying to squeeze every bit out of workers that they can. These may not be your tactics, but they are also acts of resistance.

Large acts of resistance are effective too, but remember that the media always spins such things towards Capitalist ethics. Looting in New Orleans during Katrina, the protests in Ferguson Missouri, and massive anti-capitalist marches in large cities are all examples where revolutionary acts of resistance were re-told as dangerous and criminal events.

Resist small. Consider it a spiritual practice, because it is. Start with the minor things, the things you can do easily. Listen to your body and your soul afterwards—how did you feel? What changed in you when you called off sick when you really weren't, when you made dinner for friends instead of going out for dinner, when you harvested your first salad instead of buying it at a grocery store?

What about the first time you helped a co-worker demand a raise, or marched against police brutality? Or the first time you slipped something that cost too much into your pocket instead of paying for it, or offered to watch your neighbors' kids so they didn't have to pay for child care? What about when you canceled your phone's data plan and decided to spend more time looking at nature instead of your hand, or went to a free play instead of a movie theatre?

> "One day you will be called upon to break a big law
> in the name of justice and rationality. Everything
> will depend on it. You have to be ready. How are you
> going to prepare for that day when it really matters?
> You have to stay "in shape" so that when the big day
> comes you will be ready. What you need is "anarchist
> calisthenics." Every day or so break some trivial law
> that makes no sense, even if it's only jaywalking. Use
> your own head to judge whether a law is just or
> reasonable. That way, you'll keep trim; and when the
> big day comes, you'll be ready."
> *-James C. Scott*

The more you resist, the more you'll be able to resist. And the more you resist, the more you'll be able to help others resist. Too many people fear this is the only way to live, and it doesn't help that we don't see many examples of the millions of people trying to resist Capitalism. Inspire others, and they'll have hope. And when others have hope, you'll be inspired.

Your resistance won't look like others. Try not to judge them, and ask yourself whether your knee-jerk judgments are your own or inculcated into you through education, the media, or your own fear. Sometimes we berate others who are doing something radical because we're afraid they'll fail, or because we're angry at ourselves for not being so reckless. Play with those feelings, see where they come from, and let the forests and rivers, the ancestors and spirits, the gods and the animals be your teachers.

> We have always lived in slums and holes in the wall. We
> will know how to accommodate ourselves for a while. For
> you must not forget that we can also build. It is we who
> built these palaces and cities, here in Spain and America
> and everywhere. We, the workers. We can build others to
> take their place. And better ones. We are not in the least
> afraid of ruins. We are going to inherit the earth; there is
> not the slightest doubt about that. The bourgeoisie might
> blast and ruin its own world before it leaves the stage of
> history. We carry a new world here, in our hearts. That
> world is growing in this minute."
> *-Buenaventura Durruti*

Educate Yourself

This primer was intended to give you a taste of what Capitalism is and isn't, and yet this is just a very brief introduction to the issues around Capitalism and Anti-Capitalism as a whole. Once you start to see the mechanisms and effects of Capitalism in our every day lives, it's hard to un-see them, but at the same time it's hard to see the extent of the reach of Capitalism if you don't know what you're looking for.

Explore where Capitalism intersects with both history and the present. Capitalism is deeply intertwined with many other historical institutions such as colonialism, slavery, industrialization, and the oppression of women, and these intersections not only frame our past, but our future.

We've included a brief reading list to get you started.

General
Capitalism/Anti-Capitalism:

Work by Crimethinc
Days of Love, Nights of War by Crimethinc
Spark Notes Guide to 'Das Kapital' by Karl Marx, or if you're
very brave, **Das Kapital** by Karl Marx
The Origin of Capitalism by Ellen Meiksins Wood
The Philosophy of Social Ecology by Murray Bookchin
The Shock Doctrine by Naomi Klein
Capital in the 21st Century by Thomas Piketty
Anarchy in the Age of Dinosaurs by Crimethinc

Ecology/Environment:

This Changes Everything by Naomi Klein
Defending the Earth by Murray Bookchin and Dave Foreman
Ecology Against Capitalism by John Bellamy Foster
Marx's Ecology Materialism and Nature by John Bellamy
Foster

Women/Feminism:

Caliban and the Witch by Silvia Federici
Revolution at Point Zero by Silvia Federici
Women and the Family by Leon Trotsky
Revolution, She Wrote by Clara Fraser
The Origin of the Family, Private Property and the State
by Friedrich Engels

Africa/African-American:

The Black Jacobins by C. L. R. James
A History of Pan-African Revolt by C. L. R. James
The Half Has Never Been Told by Edward E. Baptist

Imperialism/Colonialism:

The Wretched of the Earth by Frantz Fanon
The Colonizer and the Colonized by Albert Memmi
Discourse on Colonialism by Aimé Césaire
Against Empire by Michael Parenti

Indigenous Struggles:

Custer Died For Your Sins by Vine Deloria
500 Years of Indigenous Resistance by Gord Hill
The Transit of Empire Indigenous Critiques of Colonialism by Jodi A. Byrd
The Fire and the Word A History of the Zapatista Movement by Gloria Munoz Ramirez
Our Word is Our Weapon by Subcomandante Marcos

Violence/Nonviolence

How Nonviolence Protects the State by Peter Genderloos
The Failure of Nonviolence; From the Arab Spring to Occupy by Peter Gelderloos
Pacifism as Pathology by Ward Churchill

Essays:

Rewilding Witchcraft by Peter Grey
The Soul of Man Under Socialism by Oscar Wilde
On Flying Cars and the Declining Rate of Profit by David Graeber
Capitalism and the Wage System by Bertrand Russell

Video/Film:

The Educators
RSA Animate First as Tragedy, Then as Farce, Slavoj Zizek
My Neighbor Totoro (seriously)

Glossary

Means of Production

The ability to create (produce) things that can be traded or sold to others. A factory is a 'means of production,' but so is a restaurant, a café, a work-shop, or a farm. Without the Means of Production, a person has no choice but to work for someone who owns such means in order to create useful things they can exchange.

Proletariat

People without the Means of Production; basically, workers (whether they are employed or not). The Proletariat is a new class of society, created by the enclosing of common land first in Europe and then everywhere else.

Private Property

Land that is owned by individuals, rather than groups of people. Often mistaken for 'personal property,' Private Property is the 'do not trespass' sign in a forest, the fence around a field, and also the security guard or police who tell you to 'move along.' Private Property is an essential part of Capitalism, because all life ultimately comes from the earth, and if you cannot grow your own food, you have no choice but to get it from the Market.

Investment of Capital

Capital is wealth that is used to gain more wealth. The rich invest their wealth into factories, businesses, and banks where others (workers) create things which can be sold, thus bringing more wealth to the owner.

Labor

Another word for work, though with a slight difference. Labor takes on an alchemical quality, For instance, the work of cooking becomes labor when it creates a meal from other ingredients. That magical characteristic of human work is what transforms things into other things, and it's that magical force that Capitalists exploit in order to create more Capital.

Competition

The opposite of co-operation. Competition tends to occur as a response to scarcity when social cohesion has broken down, or in the absence of community. Capitalism relies heavily on feeding into those conditions, by destroying social structures, by encouraging fear, and particularly by creating artificial scarcity. Thus, the poor are always competing against each other for a limited number of resources left after the rich have hoarded the majority. This competition ensures that the poor and minorities do not unite against the very small number of powerful rich people.

Progress Narrative

The idea that things now are better than they were in the past, that humanity is 'evolving' into a more free, just, and 'advanced' state. While a pretty idea, this is only ever a matter of opinion except in Capitalism, which requires such a belief so that humans hate the past, their ancestors, and distrust less technologically-obsessed peoples. The Progress Narrative becomes a way of justifying horrible conditions in the present by stating that the past was worse, and alienating humans from the meaningful lives possible without Capitalism.

Improvement

Increasing the output or 'productivity' of land. While improving efficiency is a good thing, Improvement in Capitalism becomes an urgent demand on account of competition. Bosses are always trying to squeeze a little more work out of you, industrial farmers are always trying to extract more food from farms all to make more profit each year.

Industrialisation

A sort of 'Improvement' where Capitalists organize and concentrate the labor of others to make it more efficient and 'productive.' While on the surface seeming quite intelligent (less work for more output), industrialisation comes with extreme environmental and social costs. Smartphone factories, for instance, creates lakes of toxic waste and worker suicides

Alienation

The process of becoming detached or divorced from something. In Capitalism, we are alienated from our labour because we do not get to control what we create. We are also alienated from nature because the earth has become only resources to exploit. And wa are alienated from each other because communities are constantly destroyed through gentrification, displacement, competition, and racism.